SUPERNOVA

by Rhiannon Neads

Published by Playdead Press 2023

© Rhiannon Neads 2023

Rhiannon Neads has asserted her rights under the Copyright, Design and Patents Act, 1988, to be identified as the author of this work.

A CIP catalogue record for this book is available from the British Library.

ISBN 978-1-915533-14-2

Caution

All rights whatsoever in this play are strictly reserved and application for performance should be sought through the author before rehearsals begin. No performance may be given unless a license has been obtained.

This book is sold subject to the condition that it shall not by way of trade or otherwise, be lent, resold, hired out, or otherwise circulated without the publisher's prior consent in any form of binding or cover other than that in which it is published and without a similar condition including this condition being imposed on the subsequent purchaser.

Playdead Press
www.playdeadpress.com

SUPERNOVA

by Rhiannon Neads

CAST

Tess	**Rhiannon Neads**
Harry	**Sam Swann**

CREATIVE TEAM

Director	Jessica Dromgoole
Sound Designer	Phil Matejschuk
Lighting Designer (Omnibus Theatre)	Stuart Glover
Lighting Designer (Vault Festival)	Matt Leventhall
Set Designer	Sorcha Corcoran
Artwork	Katie Allen Design
PR	GingerBread

An extract of *Supernova* was presented as part of A Pleasance Scratch in 2016.

Supernova was first staged at VAULT Festival from 7th – 9th March 2023.

It transferred to The Omnibus Theatre, Clapham from 25th April – 13th May 2023.

This text went to press while the play was still in rehearsals and so the version that appears here may differ slightly from what is presented on stage.

RHIANNON NEADS | WRITER / TESS

Rhiannon trained at LAMDA. As a writer she was runner-up in the Funny Women Comedy Writing Awards 2017 and has written for The Imaginarium Studios in Ealing. She was part of ERA's Comedy 50:50 TellHerVision Writers Room. *Supernova* is Rhiannon's debut play.

As an actress she has worked extensively on BBC Radio, after placing as a runner-up in the Carleton Hobbs Bursary Award, including as series regular Sister Olive Hargreaves in *Home Front*. Other Radio credits include: *Vital Signs; The Master and Margarita* and *The Enchanted April* (Radio 4). Theatre credits include: *All Lies* (Alan Ayckbourn World Premiere) and *The Wind Of Heaven* (Finborough). TV includes: *Call The Midwife* (BBC); *One Day* (Netflix); *Father Brown*; *Blitz Spirit* and *Doctors* (BBC).

Rhiannon is one half of multi award-winning musical comedy duo Stiff & Kitsch (Musical Comedy Award Winners 2018), as heard on *The Now Show* (Radio 4). Their live shows, *Adele Is Younger Than Us* and *Bricking It*, were official Edinburgh Fringe sell-outs and both transferred to Soho Theatre. They are currently in development with a new musical.

SAM SWANN | HARRY

Sam trained at LAMDA. His theatre credits include: *Gulliver's Travels* (Unicorn Theatre); *Pomona* (National Theatre, Royal Exchange & Orange Tree); *Skellig* (Nottingham Playhouse); *Wendy & Peter Pan* (RSC); Prime Time (Royal Court); *The Kitchen* (National Theatre); *Mercury Fur* (Trafalgar Studios); *Jerusalem* (Watermill Theatre); *Dunsinane* (RSC & Hampstead Theatre); *Oil* (Almeida); *Powder Monkey* (Royal Exchange). TV includes: *One Day* (Netflix); *Mr Selfridge* (ITV); *Bob the Builder* (Channel 5); *The Five* (Sky); *Privates* (BBC); *Jekyll & Hyde*

(ITV); *Atlantis* (BBC). Film includes: *The Current War; Been So Long.*

JESSICA DROMGOOLE | DIRECTOR

Jessica was a theatre director and literary manager at Paines Plough before joining the BBC, first to set up Writersroom, and then as a radio drama producer. Notable productions include *Ripped* (Soho); *Just Not Fair* (National Theatre); *The Madness of Esme and Shaz* (Royal Court); *Interrogation; Pilgrim; Lost Property; Home Front* (Radio 4); *Mixed Future* (RTE); *New Voices* (National Theatre/Audible); *An Invention* and *The Drop* (Arcola).

PHIL MATEJTSCHUK | SOUND DESIGNER

Philip Matejtschuk trained and later taught at RADA. By day he lends his ears to evidence as a Forensic Analyst, and by night as a sound designer/engineer for theatre and events. Sound Designer credits include: *Wolves Are Coming For You* (Jack Studio Theatre, Standing Ovation award for Outstanding Production Values 2021); *MacBeth* (Greenwich Theatre); *The Prince And The Pauper* (The Watermill Theatre); *For King And Country* (Southwark Playhouse); *Heartbreak House* (Union Theatre); *Adding Machine: A Musical* (Finborough Theatre); *Brimstone and Treacle* (Hope Theatre – Highly Commended, 'Creative Innovation in Sound' @ Theatre & Technology Awards 2017); *The Burnt Part Boys* (Park Theatre); *Othello* (Rose Playhouse/Waterloo East/Theatrelab NYC); *Sea Life* (Hope Theatre – Off West-End Award nomination 2016); *Dead Party Animals* (Hope Theatre – Off West-End Award nomination 2014).

SORCHA COCORAN | SET DESIGNER

Recent credits include: *Edward II* (The Greenwhich Theatre); *The Replacement Child* (Hope Mill Theatre); *The Merchant of Venice* (Leicester Square Theatre); *Adam and Eve* (The Hope Theatre); *Life Support* (London Bubble Touring); *Sorry* (Kings Head Theatre, Edinburgh Fringe); *20:40* (Clapham Omnibus); *Are There Female Gorillas?* (Camden Peoples Theatre); *One for The Road, Wait Until Dark, The Reduced Shakespeare Company, Jeeves and Wooster* (Frinton Summer Theatre); *The Merchant of Venice* (The Drayton Arms); *Cleansed* (The Courtyard Theatre); *Run/Stupid People* (Cervantes Theatre) and *Baby Box* (York Theatre Royal).

MATT LEVENTHALL | LIGHTING DESIGNER (VAULT FESTVIAL)

Matt is head of lighting at RADA. Recent credits include: *A Christmas Carol* (Theatr Clwyd); *Catching Comets* (Pleasance Theatre and UK Tour); *Captain Flinn and the Pirate Dinosaurs* (Southbank Centre and UK Tour); *Trial By Laughter* (UK Tour); *Greek* (Arcola); *Turn of The Screw* (Mercury and UK Tour); *The Secret Garden* (Theatre by the Lake); *Hamlet* (Kenneth Branagh Theatre Company, Associate LD); *The Terrible Infants* (Wilton's); *Light* (Barbican, Bristol Old Vic and European Tour); *Barbarians* (Young Vic) and *The Comedy About a Bank Robbery* (Criterion, Associate LD).

STUART GLOVER | LIGHTING DESIGNER (OMNIBUS THEATRE)

Stuart is a multi-nominated and Offie finalist for lighting design. Recent design credits include: *Astoria* (Jack Studio Theatre); *Hamlet* (Southwark Playhouse); *Dr Faustus* (Southwark Playhouse); *Here Comes Santa Claus* (New Wimbledon Studio). Stuart has just finished relighting The *Mirror Crack'd* UK tour and is currently TSM for Tamasha's *Stars*.

NOTE FROM THE AUTHOR

I've been obsessed with space for as long as I can remember. It all started with a 1997 Eyewitness Planets VHS that was at my Nan's house, which took you through the solar system. I watched it on repeat. While other kids asked what your favourite colour was, I asked 'What's your favourite gas giant?'

Depression came into my life later, but just like the dehydrated space food that I insisted on getting for Christmas in the late 90s, it was very unpleasant and appeared to have no expiry date. Thankfully, I was lucky enough to have the support of my family and friends and medical professionals to get through it. (The space food). But it remains a part of my life that enjoys popping up and saying hello here and there. It's thoughtful like that.

The idea for *Supernova* came a few years after a particularly bad patch. My instinct is always to find the joke in a situation – laughter is the best medicine, after all. (Except for, you know, actual medicine). I wanted to write a show with a high-functioning depressive as the protagonist, who allows us to laugh in even the darkest moments. It explores the impact depression can have on loved ones, and the difficulties of maintaining relationships. But, above all, it's about connection (to yourself and the universe), the potential for recovery, and the possibility of making peace with the scariest corners of ourselves.

The play has worked its way through a few iterations and weathered not one, but two cancellations due to pandemics, culminating in the version you find published here.

I hope the play will speak to all the Tesses and Harrys out there and help them feel a little less alone, because I've been both. Nowadays I'm mostly just Rhiannon, which is nice.

RHIANNON NEADS

ACKNOWLEDGEMENTS

There are many people to thank: my parents for birthing me and my mum for always doing my washing up when things get tough. Alex Critoph, David Young and Will Hislop for their work on various iterations of the play. Ben Norris for encouraging me not to throw it in the bin, reading and re-reading drafts with immense kindness, and explaining the offside rule. (Not relevant to this play, but an important life lesson all the same). My comedy partner Sally O'Leary for generally being hilarious, suggesting many excellent jokes and agreeing to rehearse the 2020 version even when it genuinely seemed like the world was about to end.

The amazing team at VAULT, many of whom worked on this production too: Phil Matejtschuk, Matt Leventhall, Charlie Hazlem, Sorcha Corcoran, Katie Allen, Glenn Kelly, the disgustingly talented and so very generous Sam Swann, and Jessica Dromgoole, who took a punt on the play and went above and beyond to whip it into shape. She's a genius and I am endlessly grateful for her care and support.

The many wonderful friends who have helped this play happen in a multitude of ways.

And finally, to my aunt and uncle Jane and Tim who housed the 5 foot lino for the set in their hallway for 18 months during the pandemic 'just in case'. Tragically, mere weeks before the show was finally going to be put on, when I told them I would stop using their corridor as a rent-free storage unit, I learned that they had given it away to some people on Gumtree who needed new flooring for their utility room. It's the thought that counts.

"What is our place in the universe?"

- Eyewitness Planets VHS 1997

CHARACTERS

Tess

Harry

NOTES

Interruptions are denoted by /

Passage of time / scene shifts are denoted by a horizontal line

---

A LIGHTER

Atmospheric. It could be the surface of the moon. We're in full blown sci-fi. A figure enters the space wearing a space suit and helmet. Slo-mo. It's TESS.

HARRY, dressed as Matt Smith's Doctor Who, appears behind her.

It's not the moon. It's a street corner.

HARRY: Do you have a lighter?

TESS: Sorry can I help you?

HARRY: Do you have a lighter?

TESS: No, sorry, I'm ordering an Uber.

HARRY: Didn't know the two things were mutually exclusive.

TESS: What?

HARRY: That you can only order an Uber if you *don't* have a lighter.

TESS: No, I just mean, I'm not out here smoking, I'm just waiting for an Uber.

Beat.

HARRY: I guess I'll have to go back in and find one /

TESS: *(pointing to lighter in the cigarette packet)* Isn't that one in there?

HARRY: Yes. Yes it is. Did not know that was in there. Now I feel like a bit of an idiot. (*He lights a cigarette.*) I'm Harry, by the way.

TESS: My Uber's gonna be here in three minutes.

HARRY: That's an interesting name. Is it Portuguese?

TESS: No, I just mean I don't want you to think me rude if we start a conversation and then, you know, it's cut short because 'Piétre' arrives, and I can't keep him waiting.

HARRY: That's fine.

TESS: I just really care about my star rating.

HARRY: 4.9

TESS: 4.93

HARRY: Impressive. I only came out because they'd fired up the karaoke which would have been fine but to be honest I'm way more of a Cher than a Sonny.

TESS: …

HARRY: It's fine. We'll just stand here. In silence. It's nicer…

Beat.

HARRY: How long now?

TESS: Two minutes

HARRY: I'm gonna head back in after this cigarette anyway. Get back on the mic.

TESS: Cool, well it was nice sort of – *not* – meeting you, Harry.

HARRY: You too…?

TESS: Is that you wanting to know my name?

HARRY: Yes.

TESS: Tess.

HARRY: Yes?

TESS: Yes.

HARRY: Yes what?

TESS: Yes, It's Tess.

HARRY: Oh right, *Tess*, obviously. I thought you just kept saying 'yes'… which was really weird. Tess… How long now?

TESS: Still two minutes.

HARRY: *(Finishing the cigarette)* Well, that's… done… Send my love to Piétre.

HARRY turns to leave.

TESS: Shall do. What, 7 minutes? How is that even possible?

HARRY doubles back on himself immediately.

HARRY: I think they've put a Mamma Mia Medley on

TESS: Oh yeah?

HARRY: Might have another.

TESS: Don't blame you.

Beat.

Do you have a favourite planet?

HARRY: Sorry?

TESS: (*Louder*) Do you have a favourite planet?

HARRY: No, I heard I'm just surprised. Um, yeah I do.

TESS: Really?

HARRY: Really. Now *you* sound surprised.

TESS: I am surprised. Well, go on, tell me what it is.

HARRY: Mars.

What? What's wrong with Mars?

TESS: Nothing! I didn't say anything.

HARRY: You made a face.

TESS: It's just, it's quite obvious isn't it? Not really thinking outside the box.

HARRY: In fairness to me it is a pretty small box.

TESS: Well, if you would call the infiniteness of the universe, a thing which by definition is without end, *small*... then yeah... pretty small box.

HARRY: Alright then – what's yours?

TESS: Not a planet but a star. Betelgeuse. It sits on Orion's shoulder. It's a red-tinged gas giant around 640 lightyears away from Earth and is the widest ranging of all the semi-regular variable stars, which means that it periodically swells and then magically shrinks back down again. Plus it has a cool name.

Beat.

Mars is cool too though. That's the God of War right?

HARRY: Yep.

TESS: Could have been worse - you could have said Pluto.

HARRY: Pluto isn't a planet.

TESS: Exactly. Gold star for you.

HARRY: And neither is Betelgeuse.

TESS: ...Touché.

HARRY: I like your costume.

TESS: Thanks.

HARRY: You're a... butcher?

TESS: Yep. No, what I've actually come as is a person who over-commits to fancy dress, and then leaves the party early.

HARRY: So, wait you're not an actual astronaut.

TESS: No!

HARRY: Mind blown.

TESS: I wanted to be one as a kid. But then I had a panic attack on a forty minute flight to Inverness so I think a trip around the moon might have been a little ambitious.

HARRY: Never say never.

TESS: I think we can probably say never.

HARRY: Yeah.

TESS: And you are… Eleventh Doctor.

HARRY: Yep.

TESS: Fez is a little obvious.

HARRY: Yeh but – wait for it.

He produces the 10th Doctor's sonic screwdriver.

TESS: That's the 10th Doctor's sonic screwdriver.

HARRY: Yeah, I know but… (*He takes the cap off*) it's also a pen. Do you want to know my party trick?

TESS: Is there audience participation?

HARRY: No

TESS: Go for it.

HARRY: I can name all the Doctor Who's in both chronological and alphabetical order.

TESS: Bullshit. Chronological.

HARRY: William Hartnell, Patrick Troughton, Jon Pertwee, Tom Baker, Peter Davison, Colin Baker, Sylvester McCoy, Paul McGann, Christopher Eccleston, David Tennant, Matt Smith, Peter Capaldi, Jodie Whittaker, David Tennant, again, and Ncuti Gatwa.

TESS: You forgot John Hurt.

HARRY: Controversial!

TESS: I am, yes.

HARRY: Favourite Star Wars?

TESS: I think Return of the Jedi just nudges it because Ewoks.

HARRY: Fair.

TESS: You?

HARRY: Okay this is gonna sound crazy but... Phantom Menace.

TESS: ...

HARRY: I just think Jar Jar Binks is a very misunderstood character... I'm totally kidding – it's A New Hope!

TESS: Oh thank god! Okay, don't take this the wrong way but you don't seem like the kind of guy who...

HARRY: ...used to wear a homemade Han Solo costume to school on non-uniform days?

TESS: That is *not* what I was going for, but yes.

HARRY: So yeah, beat that.

TESS: I can't. Actually, I can. Brace yourself. As a teenager I founded and curated a conspiracy theory fan page for the TV series Lost from the perspective of the Dharma Initiative.

HARRY: No you didn't.

TESS: Yes I did. www.4 8 15 16 23 / 42smokemonster

HARRY: /42smokemonsterfangirl.com

TESS: How do you…?

HARRY: I knew that website.

TESS: No.

HARRY: I loved that website.

TESS: Fuck off.

HARRY: I submitted several fan fiction pieces to that website.

TESS: Wow. That's. Okay. That's so weird.

HARRY: Uh huh. That uber's taking a while.

TESS: Cancelled it three minutes ago.

In the scene change they undress each other excitedly. HARRY pulls TESS offstage.

Time passes. TESS creeps back onstage.

COOL COOL

HARRY: Morning.

TESS: Cool!

HARRY: Sorry?

TESS: Nothing.

HARRY: Cool? – did you say 'cool'?

TESS: Possibly. I'm sorry I don't know why.

HARRY: Okay. 'Cool'.

TESS: I think it's just coz... well I don't really *do*...

HARRY: Oh god me neither.

TESS: Oh. Right okay. Well, it was fun.

HARRY: It was fun.

He extends his hand for a hi-five. TESS goes with it.

TESS: You're kind of weird.

HARRY: Thanks.

TESS: It's a compliment! Weird-good.

HARRY: Then thank you.

TESS: Cool

HARRY: Cool

Beat.

TESS: I'm gonna leave now.

HARRY: Agreed.

HE'S TYPING

TESS is on a phone call.

TESS: Heyy! How was your night? Oh great! Yeah, mine was gooood… Caz, I think I met someone.

CAZ is clearly screaming down the other end of the phone.

I know! I know. I dunno he does something businessey I think, but he's also kind of a nerd which is very endearing and um yeah we had sex twice last night so…

Yeah I wanna see him again!

Okay! Okay… okay. So, I should wait for him to text me first?

Right.

And is that a definite rule or you know more of a guideline?

Yeah, no, absolutely. Yeah. Yeah. Yeah I texted him from my bus home. Twice. I think. So that's –

No! No, that's it…

TESS checks the messages on her phone.

Well I did send him a link to something later on but that doesn't count does it? Oh god. I also sent him two gifs. What the fuck was I thinking? He's gonna think I'm some insane needy crazy girl. Jesus Caz where were you 3 hours ago to tell me not to text him?!

Of course he hasn't replied I'm a lunatic! I don't know if he's seen them he's got his read receipts off the bastard. Do you know what I'm actually kinda mad. Coz you can't have sex with someone twice within the space of six hours and then not text them back when they send you what is actually a very hilarious link to a new Off West-End musical exploring Jedi politics called *Mark Hamill-ton*!

Okay well it says he was last online – fuck he's online now. HE'S TYPING. CAZ HE'S TYPING!

Wow he's really taking a long time to type. Proper essay, chill out mate. I mean I know I'm a catch but – Okay he's stopped typing, is that bad? What does that mean?

Oh my god, Caz. He's gone offline. Oh no that's perfect. Well, I'm dead. I'm deceased. I can never leave my house ever again.

What the fuck, now he's ringing me. On my phone. Ringing. What's wrong with him?! Well I can't that answer, can I? That's mental! What do I do? Okay, I'm gonna answer, I'll call you straight back. Alright bye bye bye bye.

She presses the appropriate things on her screen.

TESS: Hello?

HARRY: Hi!

TESS: ....

HARRY: It's Harry. From last night?

TESS: Oh *Harry*. Sorry I didn't have your name saved in my phone.

HARRY: Really? You texted me a few times.

TESS: Did I? Oh yeah, anyway. Hi!

HARRY: I wondered if maybe you wanted to hang out again sometime?

TESS: Oh. Okay. Sure.

HARRY: You don't sound sure.

TESS: Well I'm just trying to work out if you're a serial killer or something. You know, calling someone you barely know. Feels like it could be a serial killer move.

HARRY: I'm not a serial killer.

TESS: Which is / exactly what a serial killer would say

HARRY: / exactly what a serial killer would say

HARRY: Yes I know, but I'm not. I promise.

TESS: Oh, well, if you promise.

HARRY: Friday?

TESS: Uhh, let me just check I'm not busy, I think I might have plans.

TESS holds the phone away from her ear and stands there. Waits. Seems like long enough.

Yeah, no, I actually think I am free.

HARRY: Great, meet at yours?

TESS: You don't know where I live.

HARRY: Yes I do.

TESS: What?

HARRY: Look out the window.

TESS: What the fuck /

HARRY: I'm joking, sorry that's probably not funny /

TESS: / It's not funny

HARRY: I'm not gonna murder you.

TESS: Great.

HARRY: So, do you fancy going to one of the Lates at the Science Museum?

TESS: The after dark thing? Yeah could do, or we could /

HARRY: / they've got a silent disco.

TESS: You've already bought the tickets haven't you?

HARRY: Yep.

SILENT DISCO

At the silent disco. Fun. Headphones on. They are singing Toploader's 'Dancing In The Moonlight'. Badly. I'd say 60% of the lyrics are wrong.

HARRY: Are you having a good time?

TESS: I'm hating every moment.

HARRY: Cool! You're really good at dancing.

TESS: What?

HARRY: You're really good at dancing!

TESS: I can't hear you!

HARRY: *(miming)* You... are really... good... at dancing.

She laughs. They dance.

TESS: Do you reckon It'd be really weird if we took our headphones off coz everyone will be really going for it but it'd be silent?

HARRY: What?

TESS: Take your headphones off!

HARRY: What?

TESS: I was saying would it be weird if we took the headphones off coz everyone would really be going for it but it'd be silent.

They watch the room for a while.

HARRY: Yeah It's weird /

TESS: / It's really weird.

TESS: Although... (*smiling and dancing with a stranger*) I absolutely loathe what you're wearing! You. Look. Shit! Go on. Your turn.

HARRY: What, really?

TESS: Do it.

HARRY: (*tentatively*) Okay... You, sir. Your hat is... rubbish.

TESS: That was pathetic!

HARRY: Fine. Your hat is *fucking* rubbish. (*He gives him two fingers*)

TESS: Harry! They're not blind!

HARRY: (*mouthing*) She told me to do it! She's out of control!

They laugh, dance.

TESS: D'you know what. This was fun.

HARRY: (*He's already put the headphones back on*) What?

TESS: Nothing.

ENTHUSIASTIC SEX

A phone call.

TESS: He got handsome later in life, so he's gorgeous, I mean you know, you've seen him, but he grew up liking Star Trek. So every time we have sex a part of him can't believe he's actually having sex. And I'm me, so there we are, both hardly believing our luck, just fucking chuffed with ourselves which makes the whole event really very enthusiastic and I would imagine quite un-skilled.

God, I'm talking a lot aren't I?

Don't answer that. I know I am.

ASTEROID WATCH

HARRY: Okay so, hypothetically, If there was an asteroid headed for earth right now, what would you do?

TESS: Great question.

HARRY: I know.

TESS: What's the timeframe?

HARRY: You've got an hour.

TESS: An hour?! How did they only just realise that was happening?

HARRY: Government cuts. 'Asteroid Watch' was the first to go.

TESS: Asteroid Watch isn't a real thing.

HARRY: Not now it isn't. Dominic Raab!!

TESS: Okay, so, what's the level of destruction?

HARRY: Half of London is gone.

TESS: Shit, which half?

HARRY: West.

TESS: Ah well. Right, infrastructure. What goes down?

HARRY: Electricity

TESS: Okay

HARRY: Water

TESS: Okay

HARRY: Internet

TESS: Sorry what, the in – The internet goes down? How does an asteroid take out *the internet*?

HARRY: 58 minutes!

TESS: Fuck! Okay. Well, I can't watch the news. I can't watch Netflix coz for some ridiculous reason there's no internet. No water, so I can't wash the dishes.

HARRY: When do you ever wash the dishes?

TESS: Irrelevant. I guess I'd finally get around to doing that 'crochet your own underwear set' Caz gave me for Christmas.

HARRY: Are you serious?

TESS: What? Shame for it to go to waste. If the apocalypse starts, I might be grateful for some knitted undies, keep me warm.

HARRY: You're ridiculous.

TESS: Alright Bear Grylls, what would you do?

HARRY: I'd have a bag packed: water, supplies, medicines. Need to get out of London as fast as possible.

TESS: Trains are down.

HARRY: Way ahead of you. There's a zip van down the street – downloaded the app three years ago, always wanted to use it. Pick it up, drive here, come get you.

TESS: It's a 30 minute drive from yours. That's half your time gone.

HARRY: You're worth the risk. Also I reckon I could do it in 15 minutes. I'm a fast driver.

TESS: No you're not / .

HARRY: / No I'm not. I'm very cautious.

TESS: What if an asteroid was coming but we had just 30 seconds. What would you do?

He kisses her.

Well, now we've only got 20 seconds.

LIVING TOGETHER

TESS: Huh... Can I ask you something?

HARRY: Sure

TESS: Are we... living together

HARRY: No.

TESS: It's just. And I don't want to jump to conclusions here because I've never actually lived with anyone before –

HARRY: Have you not?

TESS: No, but. I don't remember the last time you went home.

HARRY: Uh... like... two weeks... no, actually – last...

TESS: Your shampoo is here.

HARRY: I've got a sensitive scalp –

TESS: And your cereal is in the cupboard.

HARRY: Makes sense for when I stay over –

TESS: What about this letter which is addressed to you at this flat?

HARRY: Oh, yeah. That is damning evidence. *(Beat.)* Are we living together?

TESS: I think we're living together.

HOT

They are brushing their teeth. She spits.

HARRY: God, you're hot.

TESS: Ha, yeah.

HARRY: You're hot.

TESS: Okay.

HARRY: Wow you are really uncomfortable with being called hot.

TESS: Harry!

HARRY: How's it going hot lips? I didn't love that /

TESS: / Never say that again.

HARRY: But I'm still gonna use 'hot'.

TESS: Oh my god.

HARRY: What is wrong with you?

TESS: Nothing! I'm just – look, I know I have a totally fuckable personality, but I'm not 'hot'

HARRY: You're fucking hot.

TESS: Yeah but I'm not lust-at-first-sight am I?

HARRY: I *absolutely* lusted after – I fancied you straight away.

TESS: No you didn't.

HARRY: Well I did.

TESS: Well you're lying. I won you over with my shiny personality.

HARRY: Your personality was like the icing on the cake. The already super hot cake.

TESS: The only hot cake I am is a toasted tea cake.

HARRY: I love toasted tea cakes.

TESS: Yes but you wouldn't fuck a toasted tea cake.

HARRY gives a look which says 'I actually might'. They're back in the mirror. Tess makes the worst face she can. Double chins galore.

TESS: Oh no, you're right I'm so fucking hot.

HARRY: You're hot! You're hot okay!

TESS: You have to stop saying that or we're going to have an argument.

HARRY: Fine. I don't smoke.

TESS: It's okay babe I won't tell the cool kids.

HARRY: The cigarette I was smoking that night was like the third cigarette I've ever smoked. I thought you

	were going out for one, in your tight little space suit, and that maybe we could bond over /
TESS:	/ chesty coughs?
HARRY:	It was the best I could think of.
TESS:	So you stalked me.
HARRY:	What? no. I –
TESS:	You stalked me.
HARRY:	Well…
TESS:	Like a predator stalks its prey.
HARRY:	No. Definitely not that.
TESS:	You were the Lion, and I was a gazelle merely trying to get an uber back to my part of the Serengeti.
HARRY:	You're missing the point here. I fancied you so much that I subjected myself to 33 known carcinogens just to find an excuse to talk to you.
TESS:	So you lied to me?
HARRY:	No.
TESS:	But on the flip side you did it because you thought I was hot and intimidating.
HARRY:	I don't think I said intimidating.

STALKABLE WOMAN

A phone call.

TESS: Yeah, so it turns out he kinda stalked me.

I am so flattered!

Come on you know what I mean. And It's fine coz I fancied him back. That's how it works.

If you don't fancy them back that's harassment, but if you do, that's love!

Fuck. Shut up. Forget I said that.

FRESH AIR

HARRY: We should go out.

TESS: Why?

HARRY: Fresh air?

TESS: I can't

HARRY: Why?

TESS: Because I don't want to.

HARRY: Why?

TESS: If we go outside we might have to talk to people and the only people I want to talk to is you.

HARRY: We should go out.

TESS: Fine, let's go out. *(Beat.)* or... or... hear me out... we could not. we could just *not* do that... what do you think?

HARRY: What do you think?

TESS: I think that sounds better.

HARRY: Fine.

TESS: Yess!

HARRY: I am hungry though.

TESS: Deliveroo?

HARRY: Okay. Thai?

TESS: No

HARRY: Chinese?

TESS: No

HARRY: Indian?

TESS: No

HARRY: Okay well why don't you suggest some things?

TESS: No

HARRY: Great.

TESS: Just keep listing we'll get there.

HARRY: Sushi

TESS: Nooo

HARRY: What then?

TESS: Yo' dick?

HARRY: Okay if you could eat anything in the world right now, my dick aside, what would it be? Go.

TESS: Packet of Doritos and a toffee apple.

HARRY: Look, will you just choose. I don't want to eat late, coz I have to be up early in the morning.

TESS: No, you don't.

HARRY: I think work would disagree. What are you doing?

TESS: I think you might have a temperature.

HARRY: Tess, no.

TESS: It would be naughty wouldn't it?

HARRY: Very.

TESS: Fun though. Think of all the fun things we could do.

HARRY: What sort of things?

TESS: Use your imagination

HARRY: …like… sex…

TESS: Yes. Sex. Yes.

HARRY: I can't.

TESS: Can't you? pull a sickie, pull a sickie, pull a sickie —

HARRY: Fuck it. One day.

ARWEN

They're playing a game of 'Beggar My Neighbour'.

TESS: Eowyn or Arwen?

HARRY: Arwen

TESS: Uh-uh

HARRY: What?

TESS: Eowyn is a total badass. She's a warrior, she defeats the possessed king, she looks fit as fuck with a sword. Why doesn't he wanna bang her?

HARRY: Coz he's already in love with Arwen.

TESS: Eugh, that's so annoying.

HARRY: What's annoying is that Tolkien named them essentially the same name.

TESS: No he didn't. *(She spells it out.)* Eowyn. Arwen. *(They sound exactly the same.)*

HARRY: Oh yeah now I see. So you think you're Eowyn?

TESS: No. I'm Treebeard. And that was a question. My turn again.

HARRY: That's not fair!

TESS: That's life! Truth or dare?

HARRY: Truth!

TESS: What's your go-to darkest thought?

HARRY: ...what?

TESS: Like, what's the darkest thought that sits at the back of your brain and whirs away?

HARRY: Give me an example.

TESS: Like... when you walk over a bridge do you have that little voice that says 'nothing stopping you, you could just jump'?

HARRY: Not really no.

TESS: Alright. How about fantasising about what it would be like to kill a man in cold blood?

HARRY: You think about that?

TESS: You've gotta know how you'd kill a man if push came to shove!

HARRY: How would you do it?

TESS: Stabbing, you?

HARRY: Erm. I guess... smothering?

TESS: You're such a pure soul.

HARRY: No, I'm not.

TESS: Oh really?

HARRY: Yeah, I'm proper dark!

TESS: Prove it then!

HARRY: Well, okay… well sometimes. Sometimes I think about if I died, what my funeral would be like.

Beat

TESS: Sorry, Is that it?

HARRY: No. Also what would people would say, and thinking about people crying over me.

TESS: You're very sweet. Dare then.

HARRY: What?

TESS: That was a rubbish truth. So you have to do a dare. Take off your clothes. Take. Off. Your. Clothes.

He does. She 'makes it rain' playing cards at him.

PLATES

Later. Calmer.

TESS: This was my best day.

HARRY: Me too.

TESS: I really like it when you're here.

HARRY: Do you?

TESS: Yeah, you fetch things so I don't have to. I don't want it to be over. I was thinking.

HARRY: Yeah?

TESS: Maybe that 24 hour stomach bug was more like a 48 hour stomach bug.

HARRY: Tess, no. I said one day.

TESS: Fine, If you'd rather be at work.

HARRY: Of course I wouldn't rather! I have to.

TESS: One more day wouldn't hurt. You're not curing cancer, you loser.

HARRY: Woah. I said no, Tess. Don't you have a shift at the restaurant?

TESS: ...No.

HARRY: You haven't been in, in ages.

TESS: Because I don't work there anymore.

HARRY: What?

TESS: Yeah, I left.

HARRY: Why?

TESS: Because they asked me to.

HARRY: When was this?

TESS: Like, a while ago.

HARRY: Why didn't you tell me?

TESS: It's humiliating. I have a masters degree in physics and I got sacked from my job at Zizzi's because it turns out I'm really bad at holding plates.

HARRY: Sure.

TESS: No, it's good actually, because now I can focus on pitching articles. *(Beat.)* What are you thinking?

HARRY: I'm thinking how bad were you at holding plates?

TESS: According to the man with the calzone in his lap, pretty bad. They made you hold four at a time, that's too many plates! Where are you going?

HARRY returns with four plates.

TESS: Oh fuck off.

HARRY: I have to see this.

TESS: Alright, bring it on. Okay so, the first three are fine *(she shows him)* but how the hell are you getting that fourth one on there?

HARRY: Oh no you're right. Impossible.

TESS: *(adding the fourth plate)* Oh no… wait… here we go… Ehhhh VOILA!

HARRY: Look – you *can* do it!

TESS: Of course I can! I'm good at everything.

HARRY: Then why did you get fired?

TESS: Get me another one. I'm gonna put it in my mouth. Go on! I reckon I can grip it with my teeth.

He gets another plate and puts it in her mouth. She is triumphant. Laughter.

HARRY really sees her.

HARRY: I love you.

TESS: Oh

HARRY: Sorry, should I not have –

TESS: No, no that's –

HARRY: It's okay you don't have to say it back.

TESS: No… It's just I'm… I'm still holding these fucking plates.

HARRY: Oh sorry. Here.

He takes the plates from her mouth and hands and puts them down.

TESS: Thanks.

The room settles.

HARRY: Okay, well. I love you.

Beat.

TESS: Yeah, no, I don't think it was the plates.

HARRY: You really don't have to –

TESS: Why?

HARRY: Why what?

TESS: Why do you love me?

HARRY:	I dunno, a whole bunch of reasons
TESS:	Name one.
HARRY:	Okay well you're beautiful /
TESS:	Shut up.
HARRY:	You're intelligent and funny /
TESS:	Stop talking.
HARRY:	Honestly this isn't me pressuring you to say you love me.
TESS:	Obviously I fucking, obviously... Are you going to work tomorrow or what?

BABY

A phone call.

TESS: Hey! I know! Just fancied catching up. Yeah good. He's good, yeah. Busy. Same old same old. What's new with you? Fuck off. Oh my god that's – fuck – congratulations! That's incredible. How long?

Wow when did I last see you? I mean I'd say we should have a drink to celebrate but... well I suppose I can still have a drink which is great. Oh yeah, yeah cool. Honestly I'm so thrilled for you both. Yes, you must. Please. Dinner yes, for sure. Okay, alright. Bye.

She hangs up.

STATEMENT WALL

HARRY: You painted the wall.

TESS: I painted the wall.

HARRY: Weren't you handing out those CV's today?

TESS: No, I went to B&Q. Bought paint. Felt important. A statement. A statement wall.

HARRY: It's certainly that.

TESS: You hate it?

HARRY: No, I don't hate it. It's different.

TESS: Guess what the colour is.

HARRY: Blue.

TESS: No.

HARRY: Dark dark blue.

TESS: No, the fancy name of the colour, guess the fancy name.

HARRY: Navy blue.

TESS: Oh my god.

HARRY: Murky pond?

TESS: No.

HARRY: Frostbitten toe?

TESS: NO.

HARRY: I give up.

TESS: Universe.

HARRY: Universe?

TESS: Universe Blue. Can you imagine, the whole universe – there it is on our living room wall.

HARRY: The universe is not this blue.

TESS: Well they were spot on with their duck egg blue, so I've no reason to suspect *fowl play*.

HARRY: How long have you been storing that one up?

TESS: About four hours. It's funny though isn't it?

HARRY: No.

TESS: Well I think it looks pretty universe-y. I'm sure they did their research.

HARRY: What, Neil Armstrong went up there with a swatch? The universe is devoid of light. Its colour is literally the absence of colour.

TESS: Yes Harry, I know that, I'm fairly sure I told you that. But it's an artistic rendering.

HARRY: Well it certainly has been artistically rendered onto this wall.

TESS: Yeah sorry, I got bored around the edges. What do you think, honestly?

HARRY: I think if you like it, I like it.

She looks at the wall, considers it.

TESS: I don't think I like it.

HULK HANDS

HARRY closes his eyes. TESS puts a set of Hulk hands in his hands.

HARRY: Oh my god these are so good!

HARRY practices a few swipes.

TESS: Punch me in the head.

HARRY: I'm not gonna punch you in the head /

TESS: Come on – punch me in the head. I know you want to! Punch me in the head!

He does. She pretends to be hurt for a second.

HARRY: Oh my god are you okay – oh right yeah.

He punches himself in the head, to check.

HARRY: No, It's fine. Okay, my turn. Close your eyes.

He gives her an envelope.

TESS: It's very thin for a pony.

HARRY: Open it.

TESS: Okay

HARRY: Well?

TESS: Ah it's a. Certificate.

HARRY: Yes, and what's it for?

TESS: A star…?

HARRY: Yeah, for a star. I bought you a star.

TESS: I don't think you can buy stars.

HARRY: Okay yes fine I *named* you a star

TESS: Oh… thank you.

HARRY: I thought it could go on the universe wall!

TESS: That's a good idea.

HARRY: Oh I think there's a message.

TESS: 'Dear Tess, the brightest star I could buy, for the brightest star in my sky.'

HARRY: I thought that would be less corny.

TESS: It's very sweet.

HARRY: Well anyway, I hope you like it.

TESS: I do. Do you know what a star is?

HARRY: Yes.

TESS: Scientifically.

HARRY: Nooo.

TESS: It's a huge glowing ball of hot gas with a temperature so high in its core that nuclear fusion occurs.

HARRY: Cool.

TESS: Essentially a massive revolving atomic bomb.

HARRY: Well, that's terrifying. To be clear, that wasn't what I was going for with this.

TESS: Its survival depends on two battling forces in constant opposition deep within its core. There's the star's gravity, which wants to squeeze the core into the smallest, tightest ball possible. And then the nuclear fuel burning in the star's core, which creates strong outward pressure. Symbiosis. It's a dance. A fight. Looks beautiful from the outside. But on the inside it's a fucking mess.

HARRY: So… do you like it?

TESS: Yeah. Did you make this yourself?

HARRY: No, that's the certificate they send.

TESS: Oh yeah of course.

CUNT / NEWS FLASH

A phone call.

TESS: How are you, you cunt? Oh shit sorry. Sorry. Hello Sammy. Yes silly Tessa said a bad word. Tell your mummy not to be mad at me. Hi, Soph, Yeah no I've got the day off so I just thought I'd – I can't really... [hear]? Are you on the hands free? I can't – I'll call back later

She hangs up. A news flash pings into her phone.

Oh my god.

She texts HARRY.

CHECK YOUR FUCKING PHONE

Tess is drinking. A little drunk.

HARRY: Are you drunk?

TESS: Celebrating!

HARRY: Did you get a job?!

TESS: Texted you about it.

HARRY: Did you?

TESS: Yep.

HARRY gets out his phone and checks.

HARRY: Oh, the black hole, I heard about that. That's cool.

TESS: Cool? It's phenomenal. They had to have eight different telescopes. All pointing at the same place, at the same time. All around the world. An

EARTH SIZED TELESCOPE. The logistics are mad.

HARRY: Yeah I know, everyone's talking about it. It's amazing.

TESS: It's really amazing. We're seeing the unseeable. We're looking into another dimension potentially.

HARRY: Maybe John Crichton'll come flying through it!

TESS: That was a wormhole not a blackhole, he couldn't fly through this. Nothing escapes a black hole. Even light.

Beat.

HARRY: Sorry I missed your message.

TESS: Okay.

HARRY: What?

TESS: S'okay if you wanna pretend you didn't see it.

HARRY: I didn't.

TESS: You did.

HARRY: I was busy.

TESS: Sure.

HARRY: I was with Pete. I wasn't on my phone.

TESS: Whatsapp has a time stamp. I know you were online.

HARRY: Yeah well coz I was messaging Pete.

TESS: It's fine. I don't care.

HARRY: I'm not ignoring you if that's what you're saying. I was just seeing Pete.

TESS: Listen Harry, It's fine if you don't want to text me but please don't pretend you didn't see the message, I'm not an idiot.

HARRY: Tess, I'm not pretending, I'm just not glued to my phone every hour of every day.

TESS: And I am? Is that what you're saying?

Harry's phone pings.

HARRY: No.

TESS: You're my boyfriend so if you text me then I text you back. I don't think that's insane.

Harry's phone pings again.

HARRY: And wanting to spend an hour with a mate without getting distracted by my phone is also not insane.

Harry's phone pings again.

HARRY: Fucking hell!

TESS: Are you gonna check that?

HARRY: No.

Harry's phone pings again.

TESS: FOR FUCK'S SAKE CHECK YOUR FUCKING PHONE!

HARRY pulls out his phone and goes to check the messages. There is some space in the room for a moment. He writes a somewhat lengthy response.

TESS: Well, you clearly take the time to text when it suits you.

HARRY: Oh my god.

TESS: Who was it? Your mum or... your best mate Pete... secret girlfriend?

HARRY: Yeah.

TESS: Yeah?

HARRY: Secret girlfriend.

TESS: Oh good.

HARRY: Bess.

TESS: Bess? That's a nice name – quite like 'Tess' isn't.

HARRY: Oh? Yeah, guess so.

TESS: How're things going?

HARRY: Pretty good actually.

TESS: Great, pleased for you.

HARRY: I dunno, she's great. She's really great, but sometimes a bit paranoid.

TELESCOPE

TESS: That's a big box.

HARRY: It's a very big box. Open it.

TESS: What did I do to deserve this?

HARRY: Absolutely nothing. Go on.

She does.

TESS: Oh my god. This is… this is amazing – a telescope! You bought me a telescope! I can't –

HARRY: Are you crying?

TESS: Shut up.

HARRY: Get it out then.

TESS: This must have cost a fortune!

HARRY: Eh *(noise suggesting 'yes but don't worry about it')* So, it'll take a bit of focusing but once it's set up the lady in the shop said even through London's light pollution you should be able to catch sight of some cool stuff up there.

TESS: This is genuinely the nicest thing anyone has ever done for me. You're unbelievably perfect.

HARRY: Nah, the universe doesn't allow perfection.

TESS: Thank you.

HARRY: You're welcome.

TESS: I love you.

HARRY: I love you too.

HARRY goes to kiss her. She pulls away.

HARRY: You alright?

TESS: Mmhmm.

HARRY: Are we okay?

TESS: Yes.

HARRY: Are we gonna talk about that at all?

TESS: Sorry. I love it. You're amazing. Come here /

HARRY: I don't /

TESS: It's fine.

TESS begins to undress herself.

TESS: Come on!

HARRY: No, Tess stop it /

She gets on her knees and tries to unbuckle Harry's belt.

TESS: I want to /

HARRY: I don't think you do. Stop. This is horrible.

He stops her. Beat.

TESS: What we need is a time machine so I can swing us back round to five minutes ago when everything was great.

	Getting hold of the required Uranium might be tricky in this political climate but if you don't ask you don't get. Do you have the number for China?

HARRY: What, just general China?

TESS: Who am I kidding? They're already listening! *(speaking to the ceiling)* Hello! I'm looking for a small quantity of U-238 but I will take U-235 at a push.

HARRY: Is it me?

TESS: No, no it's so not! It's all me. It's *everything*. It's… I don't know… I'm just feeling solitary today.

HARRY: Well, what can I do?

TESS: Nothing. You can't do anything. I just don't want to be touched by anyone right now.

HARRY: But I'm not anyone.

TESS: I know. I dunno. Sorry.

HARRY: What's up?

TESS: The universe?

HARRY: Good one.

Beat.

TESS: I'm just a bit. A bit… eugh

HARRY: You'll feel better tomorrow.

TESS: Yeah.

HARRY: Yeah.

TESS: Yeah?

HARRY: Yeah!

TESS: Yeh.

HARRY: Yep.

Beat.

HARRY: Telly?

TESS: Telly! Yes.

In the scene change HARRY dresses in an elaborate homemade Jam costume with 'Bonne MaMonstars' emblazoned on the jar label. TESS begins to put on her space suit then gives up and collapses on the floor.

JUST JAM

HARRY: Our costume is 'Space Jam'. Without you I'm just jam. There is no movie called 'jam', It'll be humiliating. The whole night I'll have people coming up to me asking what I am, and I'll just have to be like 'I'm jam. I'm just jam'. Jam isn't a film, jam is a condiment.

TESS: Pretty sure it's a spread.

HARRY: Tess, we are already late. I don't want to go to another party on my own. Again.

TESS: You don't have to.

HARRY: Great!

TESS: No, I mean just don't go and by not going you won't be going on your own.

HARRY: Right

TESS: Just stay.

HARRY: We agreed Tess – getting out of the house. It might be fun!

TESS: Those people aren't fun. They work in accounting and banking, and something called 'business consultancy'. What is this 'business' they consult on?

HARRY: 'Those people' are my friends.

TESS: Exactly, they're *your* friends, not mine.

HARRY: Wow, okay – look, I get it Tess, things are shit right now but sitting in the house like this isn't gonna make you feel better. I get down too sometimes and actually the best thing is to get up, get dressed and go see people.

TESS: Yeah, that's you, Harry.

HARRY: Do you think I spring out of bed every morning thinking 'great, another day inputting numbers into spreadsheets'. Of course I don't. But I just get on with it. That's life.

TESS: I know. I'm shit.

HARRY: Tess, don't do that.

TESS: No, I mean it. I'm shit.

HARRY: Don't shut down the conversation.

TESS: I'm a literal piece of shit.

HARRY: Fine. Yeah, yeah you are.

TESS: You should break up with me.

HARRY: Yeah I probably should. Put your shoes on.

TESS: You put them on.

HARRY: Alright, I will.

He puts her shoes on for her.

HARRY: That wasn't so hard was it? Come on then.

He stands her on her feet and hands her some wine in a gift bag.

HARRY: We won't stay long. One drink. Hellos and goodbyes.

TESS: Harry. I'm not going.

HARRY: Well I am.

TESS: Well fuck off then.

HARRY: Fine.

HARRY leaves. TESS drops the bottle and kicks off her boots in an unexploded fit of anger and upset. HARRY comes back in. She freezes, has she been caught out? He stares at her for a moment – waiting for a reaction which doesn't come. He picks up the wine bottle in the gift bag and leaves.

In the scene change, TESS puts on her spacesuit.

JAM MAN

HARRY: What have you done? The star certificate. You put it up.

TESS: Yeah.

He looks at the second framed item.

HARRY: What's that?

TESS: Oh that? Yeah that's the artwork for the latest superhero epic: Jam Man.

HARRY: Jam Man?

TESS: Yeah, Jam Man. The mother-flipping god damn one-man band Jam Man. There's a pilot episode script too.

TESS passes HARRY a script. (Scripted lines are <u>underlined</u>)

HARRY: What's all this for?

TESS: Just go with it.

TESS clicks a remote which triggers a heroic Jam Man theme.

> <u>Interior: President's Office. Jam Man and his sidekick Space Girl burst into the room. Jam Man performs an astonishing high kick.</u>

HARRY does nothing.

TESS: It does say so in the script.

HARRY attempts the high kick.

HARRY: <u>It is I – Jam –</u>

TESS: I think it says 'seductively'.

HARRY: *(Seductively)* – <u>It is I, Jam Man. You got a jar needs opening? I'm here with a tea towel and an iron grip.</u>

TESS: <u>Oh Jam Man you're so charming and attractive.</u>

HARRY: Why are you speaking in an American accent?

TESS: It's big budget.

HARRY: <u>God. Jam.</u>

TESS: No like, *goddam*. 'Godjam.'

HARRY: Right. <u>Godjam!</u>

TESS: <u>Ah we've found the next clue. It appears to be a message in a jar! How will we get it open?</u>

HARRY: Don't messages usually come in bottles?

TESS: Stick to the script.

HARRY: It's never taken me more than one go to open a jar!

TESS: JAM MAN, THE MAN WITH A PLAN!

HARRY: Have you glued this shut?

TESS: No. Say the catchphrase.

HARRY: Wham, bam, thank you Jam.

He opens the jar.

TESS: You did it!

TESS plays the triumphant Jam Man theme again.

HARRY: It was nothing. I am Jam Man after all. Now to read the message. 'I'm Sorry.' Okay.

TESS: Is it okay?

HARRY: Yeah, It's okay. Drink?

TESS: Yes.

HARRY: Drink out?

G FORCE

TESS is lying on the floor.

HARRY: Okay.

TESS: Did you know when astronauts are launched into space they're lying down? It's so that when the G-force hits them it spreads out evenly. If they were upright the G-force would push the blood away from their heads and they'd pass out.

HARRY: I did know that.

TESS: I'm not saying the pressures of my life are entirely comparable. But if it's good enough for an astronaut…

HARRY: Would you like… a co-pilot?

TESS: I'm not a child.

HARRY: Okay.

TESS: But, if you really want to.

He lies down next to her.

HARRY: Tess, what's going on? Tell me what's up?

TESS: The universe.

HARRY: Okay.

TESS: No seriously, I can't stop thinking about how big it is. I mean that's an understatement it's absolutely fucking massive.

HARRY gets up off the floor.

HARRY: Presentation went well. Did you manage to call and cancel the Amazon Prime today?

TESS: Uhuh.

HARRY: You sure?

TESS: I think I know if I did a thing or if I didn't do a thing.

HARRY: Then why is it still on our account?

TESS: Oh brilliant, well If you already knew the answer, I don't know why you bothered asking.

HARRY: I just don't understand why you can't make one phone call.

TESS: I forgot. I'll do it tomorrow.

HARRY: You said that yesterday. I'll just do it.

TESS: Don't do it, *I'm* going to do it.

HARRY: I'll just do it and it'll be done otherwise we're gonna be charged a whole extra year. What *did* you do today?

TESS: Stuff.

HARRY: What sort of stuff?

TESS: Things. Admin.

HARRY: What?

TESS: I cut my hair. Thanks for noticing.

HARRY: You haven't left the flat in days.

TESS: Because it's cold outside and the cold weather chaps my lips.

HARRY: Then I'll buy you a chapstick.

TESS: What does it matter if I don't want to go outside right now? The world will still be there tomorrow.

HARRY: Sure.

TESS: What?

HARRY: Are you gonna get off the floor?

TESS: No immediate plans to, no.

HARRY: Fine, that's fine.

TESS: Is that fine Harry?

HARRY: Yep.

TESS: I don't think you think it's fine. I think you think it's not fine, but you don't have the balls to tell me.

HARRY: Fine. It's not fine.

TESS: But now are you just saying that coz I told you to say that? Stand your ground Harry.

HARRY: Fucking hell, this is exhausting.

TESS: If you're tired you could try lying down.

HARRY: Tess, I think maybe we should talk about getting –

TESS: – Getting what? Take out? A puppy? What?

HARRY: Help?

TESS: Great idea!

HARRY: This isn't just today, this is the last three months.

TESS: I left the house on Friday. Stop being dramatic.

HARRY: Not that. This week it's not leaving the house, last week it was only eating one meal a day, the week before it was going to bed at 6pm.

TESS: The clocks changed. I was tired.

HARRY: I just think we have to admit at some point /

TESS: What? What do 'we' have to admit?

HARRY: That maybe something is… maybe you're… /

TESS: Well go on, say it.

HARRY: Depressed.

The word lands in the room.

TESS: I just got my hair cut, Harry, depressed people don't get their hair cut

HARRY: You cut your own hair, that's different, Tess.

TESS: Yesterday I learnt how to preserve cucumbers.

HARRY: / Tess.

TESS: Do depressed people pickle?

HARRY: / Tess.

TESS: Stop saying my fucking name.

HARRY: Well then stop bullshitting me. Be real. Just be a real person for five minutes.

TESS: *(sincere)* I'm sorry Harry... I guess I hadn't realised I was imaginary up until this point

HARRY: Oh for gods sake –

TESS: Wait, am I real? Are we in The Matrix?

HARRY: Fucking hell Tess.

He goes to leave.

TESS: I can't.

HARRY stops.

I can't be real Harry. Please don't make me.

HARRY: Are you joking?

TESS shakes her head.

Tess, talk to me.

TESS: I don't know what you want me to say.

HARRY: Just... tell me how you're feeling

TESS: Sad.

HARRY: Okay

TESS: Really sad. Almost all of the time. I think about... I took a knife from the kitchen last week and I sat with it for like, well it was three episodes of The Simpsons so I guess, an hour? Then I made a casserole. I used it to chop the carrots.

I flushed all the paracetamol in the house down the toilet coz I couldn't stop thinking about how many I'd need to take to kill myself.

It's fewer than you'd think. I googled it.

HARRY: You're scaring me a bit.

TESS: I'm a bit scared too. Because I think about it and honestly I don't know what would change if I did it. Coz in the scheme of things I don't remotely matter.

HARRY: You matter to me.

TESS: God, I feel like I used to be this great person and now I'm just awful and I desperately want to be her again but I don't know where she's gone and there's no way back and there's no way forward there's just this awful feeling in my body and gut and my heart and my head and it's everywhere all the time and I'm trapped, and I'm so scared.

HARRY: It's okay. I've got you.

He holds her, tries to absorb the panic attack.

We're gonna handle it together.

TESS: Oh Harry, you can't handle this.

HARRY: I can.

TESS: You cried in Wall-E, Harry. That film features 'mild peril'.

HARRY: I'm stronger than you think. I'm gonna fix this…

TESS: No. You can't. I'm fundamentally broken, do you understand? This is who I am and you keep trying to make me better but it's never gonna work and we're just papering over the cracks. You should go.

HARRY: I'm not going anywhere.

TESS: You'd be happier if you left.

HARRY: No.

TESS: Don't lie to me, of course you would.

HARRY: Being in a relationship isn't about being happy all the time.

TESS: So you're not happy?

HARRY: That's not what I /

TESS: Wow. I tell you I want to kill myself but you're the one who's unhappy.

HARRY: Tess. I am not unhappy.

TESS: No, It's fine. Who would want to be with me? I don't want to be with me. I just don't have a fucking choice do I?

HARRY: I'm gonna make you a cup of tea.

TESS: Would you stop being so nice for a second, it's making my skin crawl. How can you possibly be this nice?! I think it's probably because you're actually a bit thick. Because if you were remotely engaged with the world. With the fucking horror of it, you wouldn't be happy.

HARRY: Have you just been doomscrolling all day?

TESS: That's the world, Harry. That's the real world. Do you know I stare at you sometimes and wonder how the hell you manage to live when we're all so insignificant. Genuinely, Harry, how? How do you get out of bed in the morning when there's no fucking point?

HARRY: I don't know Tess. I take each day as it comes. Focus on the little things. If I see cherries in the supermarket, I buy them. I like holding hands and walks in the park.

TESS: You are so pathetic. I can't stand the sight of you.

HARRY: Don't do this.

TESS: Do what?

HARRY: You're pushing me away.

TESS: No. I'm just suddenly realising how basic you are.

HARRY: You don't mean this.

TESS: I do mean this Harry. I do. I have never meant anything more. I don't love you. I actually think I might hate you a bit. I think you should go.

HARRY: All I want to do is love you, Tess, but you make it impossible.

TESS: Well, fuck off, then.

HARRY: Do you know you're destroying me? You're breaking my heart.

TESS shrugs. A stand-off. HARRY leaves.

MEMORY FOAM

A voice note.

TESS: Well you won't pick up the phone so. I just want to say I'm really angry. I'm really angry about the memory foam mattress. I told you we shouldn't get it but you insisted didn't you and now, now that you're gone. The memory foam still remembers you doesn't it. I keep rolling into your fucking indentation, don't I?

I lay there last night for a really long time. I thought I might absorb you. I miss you. For fucks sake. Delete. Delete.

She deletes the voice note. Begins again.

Hello. Uh hi, Tess. This is Tess. Jesus Christ. Well, I guess I just want to say, as a reminder. DO NOT VOICE NOTE HARRY

I wonder if this is what the centre of a black hole feels like. Nothing gets in, nothing gets out. Without time. Destroyer of everything. I think about the darkness stretching out, out past the atmosphere, out into space, into the galaxy and on and on and on.

SPA TRIP

A phone call.

HARRY: Hello? Hello...? Tess?

TESS: ...Hi.

HARRY: Err... How are you doing?

TESS: I cut up your Star Trek T-shirt, I just thought you should know.

HARRY: Okay.

TESS: It was a shitty thing to do but I did it so there you go.

HARRY: Okay.

TESS: I cut between Spock's fingers. I thought it would be satisfying.

HARRY: Was it?

TESS: Yes, it was great. *(Beat)* Are you mad?

HARRY: No.

TESS: Okay. Well that's it, that's why I rang, so I guess.

HARRY: Are you okay?

TESS: Do I sound okay?

HARRY: Are you talking to anyone?

TESS: I'm talking to you, right now.

HARRY: We said we shouldn't talk any more.

TESS: Fine, I'll go.

HARRY: Don't go... Tess? Did you go?

TESS: No, I'm here.

HARRY: Tess, this is so shit.

TESS: Look, I'm fine. I'm really fine. I went to the doctor and they've given me some stuff.

HARRY: What, like pills

TESS: No, an all expenses paid spa trip.

HARRY: And you going to take them...?

TESS: I don't want to talk about it.

HARRY: I think you should take them.

TESS hangs up.

HARRY: Tess?

TESS moves away, starts a voice note.

TESS: So, there's two prescriptions. An antidepressant which I can't pronounce and a beta blocker for my anxiety called Propranolol. Proprano-'lol'. Which feels pretty fucking ironic.

Harry thinks I should take them. If he were here he'd get me a glass of water. He'd be unbearably nice. But he's not here. I'm gonna take one. I don't know why.

Fuck it. I'm trying not to lie. I'm gonna take one to prove him wrong. Because it definitely won't work and then I can call him back and tell him it didn't work and that he's an idiot and I'm beyond help and make him come back here and look after me.

NOT TALKING

A phone call.

HARRY: Hi

TESS: I thought we agreed we wouldn't talk

HARRY: You called me.

TESS: Yes, this was a test. You shouldn't have picked up.

HARRY: Tess /

TESS: I started therapy.

HARRY: Wow that's great.

TESS: Yeah

HARRY: How is it?

TESS: It's actually legit great.

HARRY: That's great.

TESS: I get to talk about myself for a whole hour and no-one is allowed to complain.

HARRY:	And are you feeling…?
TESS:	Good days, bad days. I just… thought you might wanna know.
HARRY:	Thank you.
TESS:	Okay then. I have some things of yours in a box.
HARRY:	More defaced T-shirts?
TESS:	Yeah. A really big pile. Maybe we could meet?
HARRY:	Tess.

BIRDSONG

A voice note.

TESS: Well, well, well, Tess. It's me, Tess. You probably knew that by now.

We haven't spoken in a while. I've been busy. I've been sorting through things. Not literal things. Brain things. But I wanted to say hi.

I wanted to say good job on not killing yourself. Present day me is really pleased about that. Mostly.

I wanted to say well done for leaving the house. Keep doing that. Keep doing all the work – the therapy and the medicine and the exercise and the eating fruit occasionally because I am assured it will all get easier. Until at some point it won't feel like work anymore, it'll just feel like living.

I went for a walk today. I know! And the sun was shining and I could hear birdsong. In London. I don't remember the last time I heard birdsong.

I did a little skip. In broad daylight. In Hammersmith.

You are not small and insignificant and isolated. You're part of it.

We still don't know what 'it' is. Maybe it's nothing. Maybe it all means nothing. Maybe this moment is all there is. Right now, here, in this room. Alone, together.

She ends the voice note. She puts her coat on ready to leave the house.

THE LAST HURRAH

HARRY: Tess?

TESS: Fuck. Sorry, hi!

HARRY: Hi, oh my god hi!

TESS: Hi! I already said that.

HARRY: Wow you look –

TESS: Yeah I am. Sorry you didn't say the end of that sentence, you might have been about to say 'terrible'.

HARRY: – well. You look well.

TESS: Thanks. You too.

HARRY: How have you…?

TESS: Good. I… moved. Shepherds Bush.

HARRY: West? What?!

TESS: I know. But… I like it.

HARRY: Traitor.

TESS: There's no excuse. Oh and I got a job!

HARRY: Amazing!

TESS: Science Museum.

HARRY: Fuck! That's –

TESS: Tour Guide – don't get too excited.

HARRY: Still that's –

TESS: Something, yeah. *(Beat.)* Wow. It's so weird seeing you.

HARRY: Yeah.

TESS: It's like I suddenly can't remember why I don't see you every day.

HARRY: I know.

TESS: This thing happened the other day, just something silly, and I suddenly got this feeling in my gut like 'Oh Harry would find that funny I'll just text him but oh no I can't – He's probably too busy having lots of casual sex.'

HARRY: Ha yeah.

TESS: Yeah?

HARRY: No! No.

Beat.

TESS: Betelgeuse went supernova. Well, we don't know for sure, infinite universe, time delay, obviously.

HARRY: Obviously.

TESS: Supernova?

HARRY: Something to do with stars?

TESS: Well, a supernova is sort of the last hurrah of a star.

HARRY: Right.

TESS: Do you remember how a star works?

HARRY: Two forces – this one and this one.

He shows her rudimentarily with his hands.

TESS: Yeah... ish. Well a supernova happens when the fuel in the core runs out. The star cools, the outward pressure drops. The star stops shining at that point. But the gravity keeps pushing and pushing until the core hasn't enough energy to push back any more, and it inevitably collapses in on itself. This instantaneous collapse causes the brightest light known in the universe. A supernova.

HARRY: So the star's gone?

TESS: Yep.

HARRY: What's left?

TESS: Well, if the collapse is catastrophic enough, it leaves behind a black hole.

HARRY: I see. But isn't Betelgeuse a semi-regular variable star?

TESS: Um, yes. It is. How do you know that?

HARRY: You said it once. Seemed important, so I remembered it.

TESS: Right.

HARRY: So, if it is, and my science might be off here – correct me if I'm wrong /

TESS: / Oh I will.

A ripple of recognition.

HARRY: So if it is, doesn't it mean that in its very nature it sometimes dims but then it lights back up again? Maybe it hasn't supernovaed at all.

TESS: *'Gone'* supernova.

HARRY: Gone, thank you, maybe it was never going supernova. Maybe it never will.

TESS: It was just changing.

HARRY: Yeah.

TESS: Yeah.

They smile. Lights burn brightly and extinguish.

END.

If you have been affected by the themes of this play, the following support is available:

SAMARITANS | for everyone
Open | 24 hours a day 7 days a week 365 days a year
Call free | 116 123
Web | samaritans.org

SANELINE | This is a national helpline. The offer emotional support and information for people affected by mental health problems.
Open | Every day of the year from 4.30pm to 10.30pm
Call | 0300 304 7000
Web | sane.org.uk

CALM (Campaign Against Living Miserably) | For men. They offer accredited confidential, anonymous and free support, information and signposting to men anywhere in the UK through a webchat service and phone line.
Call | 0800 58 58 58 – 5pm to midnight every day.
Webchat | thecalmzone.net/help/webchat/

PAPYRUS | Providing confidential support and advice to young people struggling with thoughts of suicide, and anyone worried about a young person by calling HOPELINEUK.
Call | 0800 068 41 41
Web | papyrus-uk.org/

SWITCHBOARD | LGBT+ helpline
Call | 0800 0119 100 from 10.00am – 10.00pm daily.
Web | switchboard.lgbt/
Email | hello@switchboard.lgbt

SHOUT | Shout is the UK's first 24/7 text service, free on all major mobile networks, for anyone in crisis anytime, anywhere. It's a place to go if you're struggling to cope and you need immediate help.

Text | 'SHOUT' to 85258

Web | www.giveusashout.org

MEN'S MINDS MATTERS | Suicide intervention & prevention specialists

Web | mensmindsmatter.org/

YOUNG MINDS | Text the YoungMinds Crisis Messenger, for free 24/7 support across the UK from trained volunteers, with support from experienced clinical supervisors if you are experiencing a mental health crisis.

Text free | text YM to 85258

Web | youngminds.org.uk/find-help/get-urgent-help/

NHS MENTAL HEALTH HELPLINES | Whether you're concerned about yourself or a loved one, these mental health charities, organisations and support groups can offer expert advice.

Web | nhs.uk/conditions/stress-anxiety-depression/mental-health-helplines/